MW00714242

The

Anatamorphosis

Sessions

POEMS
FOR THE DISSECTION OF THE BODY
AND THE MIND

Scott B. Shappell, M.D., PH.D.

THE ANATOMORPHOSIS SESSIONS. Copyright ©2014 by Scott B. Shappell, M.D., Ph.D. All rights reserved. Printed in the United States of America. No part of this book may be used or reproduced in any manner whatsoever without written permission except in the case of brief quotations embodied in critical articles and reviews.

Hekaśa Books are available at quantity discounts with bulk purchase for educational, business, or sales promotional use.

For information, please contact:
Hekaśa Publishing
7324 Gaston Ave #124
Suite 316
Dallas, TX 75214
Phone: 214-321-4158
Fax: 214-827-5292
Email: info@hekasa.com
www.hekasa.com

Book Design by Scott Baber
Cover Graphic by Travis Scott Lee Shappell

ISBN: (13 digit) 978-0-9832293-3-9

Table of Contents

Preface

Blame it on the day job (…although I always tended to be a night person). Anatomic Pathologists see and work with a lot of body parts, both at the gross (naked eye) and at the microscopic level. Regardless of further sub-specialty training, clinical focus, and/or research interest (for example, my area of diagnostic emphasis is/was genitourinary and molecular pathology and my research focus is/was prostate cancer), we are all exposed in training and work experience to the full range of anatomic pathology, from the performance of autopsies to signing out cases in surgical pathology. These run the gamut from diagnosing and staging ovarian cancers, interpreting esophageal and gastric biopsies, and performing and interpreting fine needle aspiration biopsies of the thyroid and analyzing samples of tissues and organs in hundreds of clinical and research scenarios.

Although the daily work life of Pathologists may involve a higher than average consideration of human tissues and organs, in both their normal and abnormal states, everyone has the experience of their own bodies and its various parts. In addition to individually experienced serious abnormalities, there are more frequently shared experiences of less morbid maladies and physiologic reactions under miscellaneous challenging environmental conditions. Particularly these latter have over time even become incorporated into figures of speech. Just off the top of my head (there in itself an example), I can think of several, and I'm sure readers could come up with many more. Some of these seem to be fairly anatomically and physiologically "correct" or properly oriented. Others seem more metaphorical, at least as routinely used, though they may have originated within relevant actual physical or physiological circumstances. Others may seem a bit more baffling when one stops and wonders upon the actual content and the implicated organ physiology in the context of the seemingly (anatomically) unrelated scenarios in which they may be invoked. It's always fun to learn about the origin of certain clichés or common expressions even if bits of spleen or pancreas are not involved.

As an example of the first described group, the notion of a "gut feeling" could certainly be associated with the nature of emotions and the fact that autonomic innervation and the endocrine system are activated during such states, facilitating not only certain presumably survival-promoting advantages such as in the classic "fight or flight" response, but also resulting in bodily changes that constitute part of the feeling of the emotional experience itself. In this case, those could vary from mild cases of "butterflies in the stomach," more prolonged intestinal discomfort, to acute major fright or surprise resulting in actual discharges more virtually commemorated, say, wherein a sophisticated electronic device-using human can say something like "dude… you scared the shit out of me!" Perhaps moving further along the metaphorical gamut, sometimes one may get a "lump in my throat." We often have to deal with those who are a "pain in the neck," or more severely a "pain in the ass," regardless of where or not any true physical discomfort actually accompanies the psychological angst progressing towards the frank pondering of murder.

Walking into a public restroom during a cholera outbreak is a different stimulus than walking into a bank one intends to rob and when seeing three vs. the usual one security guard noting that something "smells funny" even if one has a bad nasal-congestion involving head cold and is wearing a ski mask. The one time one of those guys pointed a gun in my face, it "chilled me to the marrow." Though I was impressed by the calm demeanor of the very pretty teller who dealt successfully with the thugs, it wasn't until I encountered her dancing at the local strip club and objectively, professionally noting some of her previously underappreciated major anatomical parts that "my eyes popped out of my head," and "my jaw dropped open" and "my chin hit the floor," even though due to my usual past reserve and/or current ALS progressive paralysis none of my voluntary muscles flinched whatsoever. Romantic fools need to remember that even more wholesome such scenarios can result in a "heartache" or even a "heartbreak," though without even mild elevations in serum LDH or other cardiac enzymes that we measure in blood as an indication of myocyte (heart muscle cell) damage. Cardiac arrhythmias, though readily clinically detectable with the proper instrumentation, are a very difficult cause of death to recognize at autopsy examination, and either way, this was not exactly what one was referring to when seeing a possible love at first site and saying later on, even without consciously detectable palpitations at the time, that "my heart skipped a beat."

When your friend (who already criticizes you for being unemployed) tells you that she (the new intended object of your affection) comes from a well to do family, is herself highly successful and you don't have a chance with a chick like that as long as you are just "sittin' 'round scratching your ass," he knows by virtue of your impeccable hygienic habits (not to mention the shear laziness that would even preclude the physical act itself) that you are not actually raking your hard keratinous fingernails over the stratified squamous epithelium of the epidermis covering your gluteus maximus. More seriously, sometimes we have "the weight of the world on our shoulders," and we need to step back and "take a deep breath" even if it is just a trip to the beach without altering respiratory tidal volume, or we just need someone to "lend us a hand" even if it's just a bit of useful information sent electronically.

The idea for this little undertaking came to me during the first Christmas holiday period following my diagnosis with ALS in April of 2009. As detailed elsewhere in correspondences and conveyed in certain dark poems[1], this has been an emotionally and psychologically challenging process in addition to the frustrating physical limitations accompanying progressive paralysis approaching quadriplegia. As noted then, if one were in need to call attention away from the physical to the spiritual aspects of one's life, ALS may be unrivaled in effectively wiping out any possible physical distractions (of the usual variety). The progressive loss of motor function leading inexorably to premature death is like a variably drawn out dismemberment, a personal trip through a real hell that's not exactly a pleasure cruise for your loved ones either.

Such a journey, to me at least, is reminiscent of Dante's *Inferno*, which indeed I revisited following my diagnosis, in the form of poet Robert Pinsky's translation of the *Inferno* adhering to the terza rhyma form of Dante's original Italian masterpiece and accompanied by haunting monotypes by artist Michael Mazur[2]. Around Christmas, then, my son Travis and I were looking at an art book featuring various illustration types by Mazur (who has had a longstanding interest in the *Divine Comedy*) accompanied by Pinsky-translated relevant short excerpts of the respective Cantos from the *Inferno*, *Purgatorio*, and *Paradisio*[3]. These illustrations were gripping and in the spirit of my own trip through hell (ALS is often described as "a ringside seat to your own demise") and my thinking that a physical deterioration might be accompanied by a hard fought enlightening spiritual journey, I thought a series of poems incorporating body parts and viscera in various settings of individual and social struggles might represent an interesting metaphor for the learning while falling apart process. Whether medical, emotional, psychological, and/or holiday spirit influenced, that night I quickly jotted down something like 27 poem titles "off the top of my head" involving certain body parts in phrases that could convey or correspond to poem themes that could in essence cover the journey from darkness to light. In the end I found myself writing poems pretty much exactly corresponding to these titles scribbled on a yellow legal tablet (ah, the good old days of being able to write - at least physically - with pen or pencil in hand).

Now, in all fairness to the reasonably physically successful evolution that's brought us from God's big bang to chief great ape on earth status, one human organ or tissue is not necessarily dark or evil compared to others. Nor are some necessarily ugly or plain while a select treasure set resemble something more like a gorgeous fairy godmother in Armani formal wear with the Pope on elbow grossly or microscopically. Yet, there are some suggestive metaphors or analogies or character castings either based on social reputation or physiologic function. For example, skin as a covering of the organism is not necessarily any psychosis induced leap of faith. Those hunters who suck the marrow out of bones know its nutrition and energy bounty, not to mention that if one encountered hell hounds of any similarity to more polite type earthly versions, they may enjoy bones, which have marrows. Most people know that the thyroid gland makes hormones that are important for regulating metabolism or energy, and its location in the neck certainly makes it a candidate target for any scenario involving a "pain in the neck." The spleen, which despite the general politically correct comments above is towards the yuckier side of organs, functions in removing senescent or malformed blood elements. Groups and policies functioning in a socially analogous manner have unfortunately not been that rare. Great poems broadening the "visceral" adjective attributes of "spleen" have come to us by true masters of the like of Baudelaire.

It's hard not to associate ovaries with women (and some poems within this series are intended to reflect negative social aspects, including attitudes that might interfere with psychological or spiritual growth, and should not be taken as an indication for any sexist or other ignorant tendencies of prejudice of the author.) As a professional physician, I have a strong tendency to associate placentas with the female pregnancy state (though of course they are structurally derived from fetal tissue, the latter which is in the vast majority of cases either male or female). Likewise, the penis (for all practical statistical purposes) is pretty much in a 1 to 1 correspondence with maleness, especially when a guy is acting like a dick. And we all have probably encountered our share of metaphorical buttholes, one of those common design features independent of X and Y chromosome distribution.

It's hard for me not to associate the liver with drinking (some may say it's hard for the weary past me not to associate anything with drinking). And of course, the heart and the brain are pretty well known for the likes of feeling and thinking (unfortunately, respectively). Et cetera. If I have offended anyone's favorite organ in the process, I hope some consolation can be gained by the claim that a completely opposite sentiment type poem could likely be written with the same tissue ingredients.

In the end, I believe about 23 poems are included that match the organ content and implications of the title from the original quickly scribbled 27 titles, though minor changes in the title may have been made to better correspond to the content of the actual composed poem. Additionally, another seven or so poems written within the usual more willy-nilly fashion that seem to fit in with the overall scheme are included. Despite a couple poems originating in reference to personal experience, certainly nothing about the specific poems or overall content is unique to ALS per se. Any unfortunate readers who may be in the throes of a terminal condition are far more likely to relate to the fact that impending death is an incredible liberator of thought[4]. Although this may be the most unique time to think and do things without giving a rat's ass (or any other mammalian body parts) about conventions, it's probably never a bad time to ponder on the less than perfect human individual or social biology. So we hope any readers may gain some benefit towards stripping away whatever barriers that still restrain each and every one of us from completely open minds and selfless loving hearts. In general, the poems are ordered to roughly correspond with the journey, something like: poems on the evil of man's misguided form; poems of hopes, dreams, and discovery; and poems of transcendent goodbye to a not completely un-noble physical companion. However, as complicated as the body is physically, any psychological, social, or spiritual process (whether including body parts or not) is even more so. As such, there is substantial overlap along any of whatever steps of whatever journey may be actually represented.

Ideally, I would have liked to been able to include complimenting illustrations as in the works that partially prompted the idea to begin with[2,3]. However, I can't draw worth a crap, nor could I when I could move my arms or had strength in my fingers. Hopefully the words alone will convey some rich sense of imagery as few things are as visually stunning, in one direction or the other, as human body parts being scattered here and there. Thanks to Sally Kilpatrick, Katy Rigler, and poet Mark Putzi for reading the poems and making comments and suggestions (other than that I report for institutional commitment right away).

Peace. Out.
scotT

Midway on our life's journey, I found myself
In dark woods, the right road lost. …

- from Dante's Inferno, Canto I[5]

"Why is it that you are ill? There is a reason for it. Many spiritual
emotions have passed through your body; therefore it has fallen ill.…
The elephant of divine emotion enters the hut of the body and shatters
it to pieces.…"

- Sri Ramakrishna, The Gospel of Sri Ramakrishna[6]

The devil always seeks to saw off the branch on which you sit. „„. The devil is an evil element. But joy? If you run after it, you see that joy also has evil in it, since then you arrive at pleasure and from pleasure go straight to Hell, your own particular Hell, which turns out differently for everyone. Through my coming to terms with the devil, he accepted some of my seriousness, and I accepted some of his joy. This gave me courage. …. It is always a risky thing to accept joy, but it leads us to life and its disappointment, from which the wholeness of our life becomes.

- C. G. Jung, The Red Book[7]

God in a Dark Suit

For the demon Amyotrophic Lateral Sclerosis

I

She sings to me again…

Tonight I feel like cutting off my legs
                    At least just above the knees
Others have it done over decades
          Sugar and pressure
          Sweet and firm
"Pay back the deal you made:
          That loan for walking on those misled roads."

I don't need a sexy surgeon
          Penis gearshift
I knew once the smithy's art
          And it can come to me again
                    In bloody book-borne ritual

Anesthesia is just a fancy phrase
          Devised for the weak gray zones
                    From which the white guards run
                    But at which the black lords scoff
When the demon shows her face
          Morphine is just so much evolutionary detail
                    Little colored sprinkles dropped
          On the nomenclature cupcake

Classification –
          Man's true opioid for the masses
Chop, Chop –
          The only one true act
Neti, Neti……

In swim the gods along the Popliteal River
          Can you fill me in such partial steps?
          Setting myself on fire seems so…gauche
                    A hopeless act best saved for later
          On the main remaining pieces

Incision…foreplay
    Extension…Stroking
        The first watchmen oozing forth
    Expecting their show alone
        To stay the flayed adventurer
Glistening tendons-like the shining sand
        On a virgin beach
"No way you have the balls," she says
        "To bust the hymen to the ex-meat
            Lipid jelly remnants of man's reddest mill."
The spinner,   the puller,   the tugger
        Gone baby gone
            My meat is gone…

You scare me not!
    A bunch of fucking bells and whistles
        I name you collagen
            I name you myoglobin
            White,   red   …whatever
                    Little spots on the dial of visible

Sever the wavelengths
        And clog the canals
      Tonight you spill not completely
I offer up in my bare hands…
        …The shiny symbol knee cap

The foolish brothers hyaline and osteoid
    Who for the sake of naming
        Spent so much of their lives
    On the ground or copulating
    With padded red or purple

Off,   off you go
  Anchor me no more
      You fragile bitches
        Who as accomplices abandoned me
          Into the recycling you go

Or into the dogs' bowl
  Would they smell "it"?
    Whatever "that" may be
      The feeder and the feed
    Monument to a transition
      Love in the flesh and bone

And tomorrow we celebrate,
        In fur and scabs aloft on exudate,
            The new stubs
        Behold the new stubs!

One more step backward to the pulp
        Do not acknowledge the soreness
        Do not lament the loss of what was lost

From the beginning...

II

What's the point of vestigial appendages?
        Ugly to the glare of the falsely grinning masses
At night the stars make love to me with their lights turned off
    By the scholars and the priests I should be coated with a warning label

The chemists want to paint me in despair
        To hide me from the rush hour parade
Tragic is a shiny mirror kept from the cursed stone
    I am not the doom, per se, just a snake made two legs lighter

I have no urge to slither on your candied landscape
        My present goal is but a partial amputation from the naming bud
            Dead headed back into a freer flopping forme frusté

"...and so - it begins," the bitch whispers...

Scalpel in the guise of kitchen knives
        And followed by an earnest blunt dissection
            The lower the parts...the lower the chains... and the fewer the stupid smiles

(ss 3/25/2011)

7

Marrow of Darkness

Six snarling hell hounds gnaw and tear
Shredding sinews off the bones, like bow
Strings of Satan's fiddle splaying in foul air
As the symphony physique of man groans low
Last legions of stretched ligamentous woe
Burst bones like sparks that fuel the red eyes' glow

One of the finest features of the proud biped
Relinquished in rupture from the drooling storm
A femur bone with which one hound has fled
To a nearby dark and quiet field forlorn
Where he'll suck the red and fatty paste, still warm
The very fuel that volts god's chosen primate form

Oh, oily source of rich strife histories
Red army drones not cursed with heads
Carrying the air we breathe in their brief destinies
To all the weapon wielding muscle beds
Shorter serving platelets swarming where blood sheds
White guard throwing flames where lowly germ dare treads

Oh to taste the bricks that kiln this mortal game
Hell's minions may just riot at the thought
To stop the bleed, stop the puss, keep the flame
For the thick blooded warriors steady onslaught
To savor the core of the White Knight's demonic lot
For nothing down below can match what man has wrought

(ss 3/16/2010; 10/09/2012)

8

Evolution of the Master Splenic Filter

I

Oh you misfits, harlots, darker skins, and thinkers
You gentle dwarfs and rejects of the master plan
What heart-felt voices sing their tearful hopes for you?
The Baudelaire hymns of praise for the browner elements
The wolf-bitten McCullers' humble prose of outcast tolerance

You slightly-offs, not hypnotized but dreaming still
You drinkers of the true intoxicating wine of spirit
Malformed and malfunctioning reminders all
Of the complex fate that could have stricken
Each loud chanter of the Spleen supporters

Their unquenchable thirst for conformation
Hardens their hearts, and blood from stone
Cannot disquiet the red and white pulp
That wields the ax of social justice
That chops and ingests the weak and the dissimilar

II

The purple people eater really does exist
A massive pulsing spleen oozing down the street
With a swagger that only the pomposity
Of a mindless organ drunk on its own authority
Could merrily whistle with as it blindly stumbles on

In visceral majesty the sweeper moves and eats the frail
Blotting its unholy juices to white-wash mask the whole
While drowning not just Noah but even all the rest
In the rotten wine fermented only from the ripest
Fruit of pious seed picked through the rank majority

Rolling like a giant fleshy ulcerating mass arisen
From the ancient loins of Hypocriteous
Growing in darkness like the coldest ball of snow
Bathed in stolen or self-appointed righteousness
Its hilum cave the endless pit of ignorance

III

Worshipped by the mob insatiable
At the absorbed cost of their starvation
It has lived and thrived since primal times
Transfigured in our age and mated with technology
Bastion of grade-A purity maintained at any price

The failing putz of the Beer Hall *Putsch*
Arose and spread the pulp like an addicting black malignancy
He took the throbbing pre-spleen of collective bitterness
And grew the red-hot monster poisonous
A well-nourished succubus feeding on the hatred of all time

Hail The Great Black Spleen, The Genocidal Organ!

Down the boiling canals tainting off demonic steam
Passed the hopeless to their horrid planned and acted on extinction
Through a group psychosis sieve of imaginary genes
While metal splenic pseudopods cast in the form of Stukas
And ever larger Panzers feasted on thy neighbor's corpuscles

IV

The so-so Koba would set a new benchmark
For homogenization by Splenic feeding frenzy
On those who just didn't feel like partying in style
And used the accessory Spleens of trains and bullets
To rid a new lowest common sad denominator of its pesky thinkers

And empty gullets air the trumpets of the Splenic Lord
Mindless, heartless melody of lauded new regimes
Better to be uniform way down at the bottom
In suffering, we shall have at least the comfort of our sameness
Better red, cold, and hungry than anything neuronic

Hail The Great Red Spleen, The Organ of Oppression!

Soon the dreaded tremors of the Splenic iron hammer
Methodic and efficient filter of power-lust disguised
As a Bear to feed and fur her simple cubs, turned into
A cannibalistic hell of informant brothers that even slaughtered
Plant genetics while strangling the crops to feed its other body parts

V

But yet it roams today in the costume of a pretty capsule
Approved by Egos and funded by your taxes
Squashing with enthusiastic glee as it politely
Gorges on and on upon the forms of undesirables
An appetite for all materials it spreads throughout the land

The great mother Eagle even feeds the baby spleens
In far off deserts and exotic jungles of the future marketplace
While breathing inside its deepest and most buried layers
Pigmented cells fill the concrete islands of despair
Trying to stand tall when strange legs are but a Splenic delicacy

While the blessed percentiles are protected
From the never welcome no-matters by the comfort
Of the peephole blanket of the news machine and the magic
Of the special language of the highest Splenic cult
Spoken beneath the sacred dome upon the detached hill

Warm words by the wielders of the Spleen's inertia
Who for the service of staying at the Splenic summit
And as further strength against the dreaded wings of thinking freely
Come in just two highly counter flavors: simply red or blue
The colors of the Splenic innards when looked at with the microscope

These great animated statues with brains forever granite fixed
Will stamp out all the un-fit-inners to take away unlikeness fear
Or else hide from us these so pesky outside lights
Under the magic cloak called "programs"
That simulates the sheen of true acceptance and concern

The great homogenizer has evolved
In the warm embracing Spleen with golden cross upon its hilum
Meddling its steady war against the dread of individuality
Led by the intolerable fake smiles of red pulp insecurity
And the drowning hemorrhage of misdirection information

The treasured Splenic Handbook gives the iron rules
By which we properly can fear the only approved God
And how to execute forever the eye-gouging of the blind
It explains why the Y's cannot be used with other Y's,
That XX + XX is not a valid sum, and Even Rules for Art

The Great Projector of society will then update
The codes for our expected forms of worthy sameness
Through glossy images of air-brushed real perfection
And numbing electro-therapy of the loud distraction plan
And give the criteria by which we note the Splenic food

Hail the Great Red, White, and Blue Spleen, The Organ of Lobotomy!

The brainwashed drones of dogma look upon
The strange like a plague of clever alien design
To destroy the sacredness of mediocrity
While going to the Splenic Temple to firmly mechanize
The Christ as the gauge for scales of fear and ignorance

The mass that turns its head for deviation is the polished Spleen
It spreads its meatless pulp in the honor of the closing mind
Its hot red lips phagocytize the standouts subtly
As the United Purple Front marches o'er the land of the free
Preaching its soma of uniformity in the guise of the mantra:

"All Like One and One Like All"

(ss 3/18; 9/20-24/2010)

There's Too Much Thyroid Juice on the Guillotine

It must be something magical to kill a man!
If God gives life, tis this that steals his power
Try to stop just after one, if that is you can
Before Hell breaks loose into the thyrotoxic hour

To stab or shoot or choke can show
Your mastery of form in splendid execution
But beheading sets your kindled mind aglow, so
Thank the Dark Gods then for war and revolution

Hard to chop a body into two, you understand,
At the level of the neck with some precision
Without slicing through that magic gland
At something more than every now and then

Under leathered skin, throbbing like a beefy gullet
Hanging like a shield before the voice
Front and center, bulging in defiance of a bullet
Noose won't spill the juice, leaving you no choice

Keeper of the fluids of the life-force
Master of the other endocrine pedants
Too little, cold, fat, sluggish, coarse
Barely worth the blade, those sloth-like miscreants

Ah, but to be intoxicated with excess
All the rage for a psychotic pre-dictator plan
Hot, energetic, little need for rest
Lovely attributes for a military man

With a sense of the poetic, nostalgia in the breeze
Take thy opposition to the guillotine in ones and twos
Glistening, razor sharp the blade cuts through with ease
Hopelessly the head goes thump into a basket full of ooze

As the bodies pile the blade grows slightly duller
Yet more effective now at roughly shearing
Soft tissue fragments on the crowd, made fuller,
Where every smear upon a face brings cheering

Hormone of energy and fire drips upon
The killing planks, slowly forms a trickle …
Then a stream, weighing on the dusty ground
Tis not Death but man in mobs that wields the sickle

(ss 3/17/2010; 10/10-11/2012)

13

Lips: A Myth of Exodus

Soft,   purple,   sensuous
          Gateway to the fragrance of kisses
Hot,   red,   passionate
   Veil   to the   columns of teeth
Keeper   of the   hidden tongue
   Alight with these to hold or to unleash
          The powers of beauty or of blackness

Sling the weight that sinks us
          In our selves
Blow us out into the storm's
          Shared nothingness
Laugh and layer us within
          Mass comedy
   To hide the truths unrealized

What should be the lyre of God's wisdom
   Krishna's karma megaphone
          Is far too often just the babble bubbler
              Of bandages to balm the ears'
          Inevitable heartbreak and despair
              The horn that harks horrific
                  Fanatic cries and racist rants and orders for the charge!

Words float through the darkest crimson
C r e v i c e s like thick night mist d
                              e
                          s
                          c
                              ending
          More fatally than mustard gas into the
Tr_{enc}hes of a gasping thirsty populace
What should be the final orderer of out flowing
      Glory of an Aria of oneness and compassion
          Is much easier to use for the commands
That load the trains to Auschwitz

Not a prayer, just a scream

(ss 3/16/2010)

Forked Penile Illusions

You say one thing but mean two other trickeries
And with protruding tongue in rite to Bifurcation
Your hot breath a mighty wind that parts the sees
Leaves islands in the chaos beyond the hope of navigation

You take the three and place them here
And you command each part to suit your will
You put the fourth and darker ones elsewhere
And in the power of your grand sac hold still

Firmly in the false pride of the myth of wit
You display the always swelling dorsal vain
And in the action of the circle left inadequate
The great splitting spitters discharge disdain

You feed the mighty mounds of so low glossal meat
And fill the spaces cavernous with your hot elixirs
And with the syrup-coated lava of your thick deceit
You blast the one into a mass of turbid haters

No wonder you so often miss the gentle rise of middle
You dance around the whole and lick a storm on either side
You miss the nectar of the Earth on which you diddle
You fear the pit inside the peach so smash the fruit instead

(ss 11/14-17,20/2010)

The Sealing Anus of Mentally-Constipated Black Holes

Time and time again, like pressured regularities
The orifice of those big heads above the necks that hold
Our biggest medals will pronounce the end of big discoveries
From now on just fine details, like science spices, we are told

To save themselves from future Immortalized
Morondom, those great masturbating minds
Trying to leave the masses mesmerized
Should refrain from claiming Final Finds

Sometimes those who seem so famously to be
Our most worldly-treasured brilliant lads and lasses
Are full of just enough warm bovine fece
To give each of us brown-coated glasses

Enough manure to fully fill the courses
Of all Earth's valleys and their branches
Where if closed-mindedness were horses
Most us folks would own big ranches

Hot air where if pronouncements could turn fans
Within those hallowed halls that echo grand naivetés
We'd have energy for all, and when they'd sit on cans
These over stating ego slaves could all shit batteries

Talkin' all that's dark and stinky ain't awl (oil) … or even coal … blues:
There'd be no more world hunger… gas would cost 50¢ a gallon… we could pay off
the national debt… and everybody else's too… there Would be such a thing as
a free ride.. ..there'd be no need for tax breaks… 'cause there'd be no need for
taxes… strippers would only have to take tens or greater in their panties… we'd
vaccinate against apathy… world-wide… double doses… things would be
swell… all over

Giants are for standing on their shoulders
Not for putting in the square behind glass shields
For placing silent peasant lips on cold hind quarters
So much so that they forget to plant the fields

Freud, the master, whom still these days we know
Finds too much fame because sex sells eternal,
Wanted Jung to simply propagate his own libido
What an ego!, and boy, you talk about "anal"

What's a bigger sign of a bigger big-head drone:
Thinking you have all the answers quite spot-on
Or trying in advance to not let anyone
Else think differently in case it is you don't?

While Breton was waging war on Dalí trying
To convince him that the only way to change a man's
Mode of thinking to an open mind was by applying
His specific method solely and to do it just like him

Hitler's Lightning War was taking Surrealism to
A truly global level, for something very bad
Is 'round the corner when they who want control of you
March down the boulevard black uniformly clad

The pectinate line separates the undulating
Hills and valleys of a propagating dark foul source
For maximally butt-tightened brain-washing
With propaganda aliquots to stink the world on course

For the self-anointing sphincter holding tight
So the "My way or the highway" seal won't rip
Without the fist for freedom to introduce the light
That great dogma cave may burst and turn the world to shit

(ss ~2/2011; 10/2012)

A Man Meets a Placenta in a Bar

Cock tale held in your fat fingers throbbing with gametic fusion
I sip in humors while you pulse with life's fluidic promise
You make me squirm in a tough spot of cosmic confusion
Fool me once, shame on me: the lustful gardener
Fool me six billion times, shame on reproduction:
Copious corpuscular copulation lured by your Darwinian glare

Your blunted cotyledons, like Medusa's shaven crown
Sweating sessile temple dark, fountain of conflicting sacrifice
Purple bag of life, all masked in smiles and breasts
Are you still the cat burger of Mother Earth
In a landfill heaped with the rejects of the race you fed
Ironically anchored next to an empty box of tampons

I want to know, dripping demon of dark red mystery:
For what purpose doth thou from your bed new man expel
To chase the cave-like entrance of your prized domain
To harden the clay with thoughts swelling in the growing gray
You protected with your top-secret magic filter
As if answers could come to the puzzle of viscera
You slowly pieced together like moistened lumps of Shakespeare

Instead, I think you pass on suffering, as some disc-shaped
Vigilante harlot on the prowl from a cult committed to misery
Like a country western song sung through a bucket of amniotic fluid
You smell like sex but taste like time's historic heartbreak
A drop by drop torture from the daily veins of strife and toil

But, in the end, I guess I have no choice but to go home with you
To hold tight to the dried out rusty fragments of our biologic fate
So I grab a'hold of those once mighty cords that joined us all
And pull up on the stool that's always next to you
Try to place my belly close to yours and whisper through
The smoky membranes, "Can I buy you a drink?"

(ss 5/28/2010; 10/12/2012)

The Shepherd

They take their sacrament of stew and loaves
And lay their little lambs to sleep
With one eye braced they watch for wolves
While against the grain and through the moon I creep

As they loiter lidded on the feeding hill
I slink down to the swamp and chant my primal call
They dream the Angels soma to keep the beasts all still
While in the deepest darkest mist I join the Witches Ball

Tonight the mistress coven seems to make their point
For to cut blood's path anew they did bring their sharpest blade
With no need now for Newton, they pierce my shoulder joint
While flailing is for trembling cults, it flees the pact I've made

With the dawn my rousers dab the dew upon my brow
Through the shade of blood-shot eyes that tear my loss of sun
I gaze at wool and song but crave the blackened earth to plow
Midnight finds me begging butchering again, careless of mutton

(ss 3/26; 4/4/2011)

Hands, Nuts, and Other Interchangeable Parts

A familiar friend acting normally, maybe at the
hardware store, is a good thing The scary stage of life
should be well propped We shake hands and make the
ritualistic appropriate   small to medium talk
Share details about   presumably important
projects that could   fill up to weeks of time
on the empty calendar   of the Here and Now.
Our hands gesticulate   as we converse, adding
an optimistic element   of drama to the rational
realism of the ignored   inexorably progressing
precision of the cesium   clock; helping to confirm
our describable position: right there, in aisle 9, seemingly safely
grounded at the intersection of x, y, z, and time t from when
our hands first grasped the feeding breast.

Some fastened units that link us
securely back through Normandy,
Napoleon and Newton and forward
to the barbeque at Norm's next
Someday. We wave a subtle and
manly bye to acknowledge to our
Friend his role, and watch those same
hands nimbly grab the nuts and bolts,
New paint, new trim, new molding
to provide the needed façade of change,
Of progress. But over the parameter of
time (was it weeks, or months, or years?),
The conversations changed. In drifted
a scent of increasing out-of-tune. The
Comforting worldly endeavors of our
prior peer seemed to fade. The concrete
Makers of concrete slabs on comfortably
concrete planet needed someone else with
Whom to hit the small white ball; to discuss the ins and outs and rounds of
Hardware. And in passing wonder as fleeting as a birdie: "Whatever happened to what's
His name?" As no one ever writes the   sequel to: "He dropped off the face of the Earth"

(ss 5/30, 31/2010; 10/14/2012)

The Course (Visions and Olfactory Cues to the Falling Apart Blues)

I stepped outside my self a while
As That's what everyone was into
And I really had no choice
Given all the smiling guides

I danced to the right all day
As That's the way their music moved me
And they took me to a grand ballroom
Ornate and lined with glossy mirrors

I don't think they worked quite right
As they reflected just selected rays
And it took what seemed a real long time
Stripping them at last to see the underneath

I tinkle on myself sometimes, not a lot
As a little is enough to leave a scent
And teach me later things don't work so well
Decaying parts and mind and sense of self

I am a freak who now lost everything
As much of that as what I never really had
And the real truth wafts up between the patches
Giving nothing to look forward to

(ss; 1/11/2011)

It's Not a Callous, It's a Cave

He threw convention to the Party wolves.
His parents were confused.
Without remorse he said a warm
Goodbye to the land upon which
Sets the sun,
But there is no flicker of a light,
Where the all night fluorescence
Of the old factory bulbs
Casts the inner security
Of a vacant strip mall.

Through the land of ancient rishis
And recurrent dysentery, groping for
The inner strength of sages,
Losing dead weight from past ages,
He walked on sandals rotting like
The fading myth of outer comfort
Village to another village
Where the humble offerings
Of the locals sustained his corpus
And fed his craving mind

Bathing in the magic rivers
That sent his testes into his tonsils
He cast his clothes and then his shoes
Into the wetting cleanser of the earth
As he pressed forth towards the call
His reddening feet struggled
To the edge of common humans
Into the jungle his roughened heels
And ignoring toes led him along
The thinner paths, unto the end
Of all things flat; the permanent
Farewell to all things level

The monkeys laughed, but showed
Him what to eat, as he stumbled
Through the thickness to grasp for
Leaves and berries, they jumped from
Branch to branch, ever higher, showing him
His limitations
The snakes gave wide berth,
As to a fledgling eagle

Finally, up the rocky oft hidden
Trails, into the secret prominences
His thickening keratinous soles lifted
His down-scaled upper form
Forever higher.

A rare yogi would pass him
On this most barren highway
The matted hair and gentile smile
And tattered robes, a benediction
Giving him more knowledge
Of the stars and touchable sun
Than any conversation between
The thousand language differences
Could impart

Up the rocks, his equally
Granite feet slowly flew him
Among the hallows of the mystics
Carved by Indra into the highest
Reaches of Himalayan Mother Earth
Oh sweet altitude
Giver of polycythemia and absence
Of the groveling hordes
He entered the lumens of the dark solitude
Where one does not look inside
One simply stops looking outside

And rests his weary callused feet
And absorbs the bliss of God's
Great Caves

(ss 3/22-23/2010)

Liver of Dreams

And Malt does more than Milton can
To justify God's way to man.
Ale, man, ale's the stuff to drink
For fellows whom it hurts to think...
　　　　　 - A. E. Housman, "Terrance, This Is Stupid Stuff"

What kills the common good man faster?
The plow he gnaws the harsh earth from behind,
The shovel he spoons the coal into the flames,
Or the poisons he laces into his heart and mind
That keeps him beastly pressing on and on

How do we know a decent man is dead?
By the dull eyes of the stare of crush,
By the breathless lungs of fibrous chest,
Or when he no longer sings romantic tales:
Dreams pronounced in lubricated pub bravado

The mist of exhaled smoke hangs densely in the
Stale and pungent air flavored with testosterone
And the dried sweat that earned the knightly pints:
The ales and stouts and lagers of the working warrior
Pilsner, better muse than pills for red necks collared blue

If we weren't supposed to drink the malted nectar
Why did the Lord who gave us hungry bellies
Also give the tools to break down our spirit fuel
Ah but that fine line we humans must uniquely tightrope
Too much, and the scars rob our futures and starve our children blind

(ss 3/28, 31/2010)

Ovary Poor-boys and Other Anthropological Mishaps

Oval, pink-gray and glistening
Fairly moist when first removed
Or if kept a certain way in saline
Slippery, but not completely smooth
Finely irregular like a gentle moon
From a variable life span of ovulation

Good for breeding, that's for sure
Lucky that they come in pairs
Jacking-up the odds of shooting aces
From the club head master ejaculator
While the keeper of maternal pantry
Offers sharing of her belly incubator

Like an oyster in appearance in some ways
Although perhaps a little small if one
Were truly trying to make a sandwich
You'd like maybe six or more
Ah, like the good old days, when it was fine
To have as many of their bearers as one could

A collection of wives with a collection
Of ovaries, there when you need them
Silent all the rest, like a good hunting dog
Except, they shouldn't hunt, or make war
Certainly they shouldn't vote and never rule
If you can't actually eat them,
You at least don't want their kind
Throwing spicy sensitivity into the mix

(ss 3/17/2010; 10/28/2012)

Seeds - A Prayer to the Cosmic Wombs

Locke sank into a swoon;
The Garden died.
God took the spinning-jenny
Out of his side.
                    - W. B. Yeats, "Fragments"

I

Virgin, touch my trembling heart
        though I don't deserve your soft caress
Love me even though my past
        dark misdirections rise to guard me
Penetrate my prideful reason,
        burst the rigid bronze of my false fortress
Strip my self-imposed confusion
        and purely help me now to see

II

Wisdom, mistress of the rocks
        and trees, embracing Mother of us all
Walk me through this human
        desert with its burning blinding finery
Guide me now into the forest,
        along the stream up to the water fall
Reveal the rainbow's magic rays
        of love beneath our man-made foolery

III

Rhada, teach me how to love
        with strength that rises past the stars
Devotion with a greater force
        than the grasp of all our silly snares
Show me a path that will
        transcend the daily pain and scars
Light me to a glow divine
        immortal love past earthly cares

(ss ~01/2010; 3/18/2010;10/2012)

Coup of the New Math

In parts of the castle we always thought we'd hide,
I am immersed within the ones who add to me.
Let x = my ability at any given time called t,
Let y = the sum of all the efforts of those parts outside,
Then $y(t) \geq 100$ percent old me – $x(t)$.
No one knows how to express x meaningfully,
Yet y is so proficient at filling in axiomatically.
A bad student at long last, as it's the old form I try to be
Instead of learning as I watch y swelling in the whole
     and becoming a good small component of the Total.
It is as if a war were waging in a theater that few could see:

     The Old Guard brought its well-known cavalry
     With its seemingly unlimited supply of ATP
     And an infantry polished to the precision
     Of maximal effort by so many a past excursion
     Commanded by the doubt-less General Mind
     Undefeated forces surprised by a new fighting kind
     And when the rebels struck so well at each division
     The Old General had no choice but full concession
     To the incomprehensible demands of these
     Unnerving small component revolutionaries

(ss 01/15-16/2011; 10/30/2012)

Fading Footsteps in the Sand

He made happy, silly dance steps
On the asphalt playgrounds of innocence
Steady stumbles over daily grinds and friction
With only the handbook of the insecure
As a guidebook to the great distraction

Time, cruel box lid on the Newton world
Maps and coordinates placed him
On a Swiss-made finite stairway
Gold-plated hand-me-down
From many hollow myths and legends

He walked for a long time … a very long
Long time on anti-septic painted
White washed tiles of halls of hospitals
Where emergence met the stage
Without a warning

But now, that hidden wind fillets the laces
Of his shoes and from his gaping chest
The pre-scarred Virgin soul leaks and flows
Down ancient rivers of dried out veins
To the soles of his cracking feet

Each blade of grass caresses new found toes
Like uncovered texture of a breast
Moisture from the still unknown
Ascends within compliant air
Like long lost ladles to his thirsty lips

At cliff's edge he pauses frayed
Tattered form blurred into the roar
Of ocean vast, where the ancients
Buried in the stones claim that mighty
Whales once came here to die

Gentle giant forms of peace in shallow
Waves, rinsed in bubbling foam
Of the long waters last few steps
An unseen arm around
The fragile waist of mammals

He draws it in because he wants
To know soft whispers one can't hear
Noted with the subtle organ
That picks up the sun
And the passing of the forms

He descends a path that's clearly
Labeled by the Moon. Balls of his
Wizened feet caressed by knowing rocks
Shaped by ancient waters, softened
By the breath of all the planets' dances

Walking on the dwindling warmth of patchy
Moonlit sands of the beach at the end
Of the world where the salt of deepest
Mountains mixes with the most polished
Elements from our Great Mother

To form a velvet carpet to the next beginning
He acknowledges what lies beneath
And looks upward, his eyes now
Blissful tentacles, toward true knowledge
Where the stars wink their loving welcome

(ss 04/11/2010; 10/13/2012)

My Most Sensitive Parts

My dogs can smell a squirrel from
Thirty yards away; I'd be lucky to
Sniff one if it fell upon my face.
When I bury my nose-in-training
In an aged Bordeaux though,
It is I and not they that get to
Pour the magic liquid earth
Over the tongue that knows how
To shop at the liquor store,
The one with thumbs.
After all, the one dog that can
Smell cork taint I can't detect until
I taste, also eats cat turds from the litter box.
Just how discriminating can he be?

My cat can hear a bug crawling
From across the room, but it wasn't she
Who made the funds to decorate it.
Were my ears made for shouts
Of the marketplace, car horns
In the traffic of the disconnected
And unmoving,
Or for a symphony of Brahms,
Or for the softest whisper of the
Ancient wind blowing over the ground
At Mesa Verde, which I barely heard?

After all, we are visual beings
Hence, the highest praised neo-cortex
Yet, when I read Rilke and Neruda
My eyes are still so incomplete
There's something yet I've not unleashed
A gift shared with cats and dogs and crawling ivy
Something deep, my spot most sensitive
I close my eyes; I try to shed my brain
The unnecessary fortress
And reach out into the awesome void
The larger side we cannot see
And from which we mostly hide

Lilac blossoms shower from a nether tree
And softly land upon the absent skin
Of my degenerating and extending arm
A tender foam-*espuma*-
Dissolving all of me into the ocean
Like a jar of prior unfulfilled
Potential crystals
Filling my shedding eyes with purple ether
Concentrating a universe on one of its essential parts

(ss 3/20, 22/2010)

On Any Given Elbow

The preacher removes his glasses and solemnly
Rubs with his left hand his eyes (always searching,
and sometimes seemingly so powerless)
While his right hand holds a pencil, questioning,
And both his arms rest on the desk his father's father
Owned, a fading fire in the hearth and a loyal
Dog resting on his own old and calloused forepaws
The Lord is being more resistant on this night
His sermon not forthcoming despite the prayer
As if the older he gets and the bigger
The queries are, the deeper the Good Lord hides

Young men fall, old men fall more often
For reasons only the Lord and the inventors
Of quantum gravity can begin to understand
Some downed men will always try to rise again
So tired, from reaching up over and over
Last grasps, like a senior soul in a sweat shop
Her age-spotted thin determined hands
Placed patiently, patriotically to her sewing machine
She braces herself, hands to wrists to shoulders
Of loyal arms, faithful; and raises the fragments
Of herself to face another day of unknown merit

Preying hands: the hunter his bow doth draw
His thin but muscled forearm in tendonous
Camaraderie with firm wrist and purposed fingers
And in fusion by the masterful hinge
With a mighty and painted bicep, holding the
Promise of the food of the future and the ink
Of a glorious past: his family, his people, his gods
Praying hands: sacrifice, anguish, and adoration
All on the same stand of upward humble posture
All the routes to survival, all the paths to heaven
Pass through the humerus connection

The log in the fire, the spear in the side
The chipping of stone, the mounting of wheels
The saw through the log, the paint on the fence
The sowing of seed, the harvest of grain
The hands on the utter, the hands on the fetus
The needle through the cloth, the suture in the wound
The scribble of the pen, the stroking of the brush
The hand on the throttle, the push of the button
The row of the oars on the lifeboat of humanity
We pass from here and everywhere to there
On any given elbow

…and the old man begins to write…

(ss 6/16-17/2010)

Earwax Submarines

For the cortical cleansing of a lifetime
Of empty Elephant and Donkey song
So removed from the Nature
Of animal presence
The irony is that past sad

Aural instillations from the
Self-anointed demigods
Who float gloriously
On all the sonar bandwidths

The new Goddess Media
Locked her sister Sophia
In a military prison of unknown IP address
Guarded by the drones of
Miss Information Technology

Meshwork of paraffin plugging canals
Greasy yellow giving way to agent orange
The pathway of words now by-passed
By the perpetual glow of plasma
Augmented by the rubber ear-buds
Of the unplugged
As effective as a lifetime of
Otosclerosis

How do you penetrate
The impenetrable barrier?
The persistent reinforcements
From the mighty ceruminous glands
Like the Czech hedgehogs on the
Beaches of Normandy
Must we lose everyone
At the cost of Truth?
Cerumen! Cerumen!
Mighty Cerumen!

A Trojan Horse just simply will not do
It's far too archaic, no part even nuclear
Although a heaping dose of oral Homer
Would make a healthy supplement
Later in our plan

We need something dark
A tool covert and submerged
A thrust from underneath
Something of the Primal waters
Torpedo force to make it through
The sticky barricade
Mushroom light to clear the clouds
Perhaps an enlightened fleet
Of Earwax Submarines

(ss 4/08/2010)

The Plaque Wall

For Ralph

For an amplitude of service that truly can't be measured
Like a long hallway lined with dusty photographs
On which you need not worry small details
As we are your collage of a lovely village dance
That only a fool cursed far worse would ever call a tangle

Caught in a flow of infinite directions
On each divinely mapped out coordinate
You took to heart your place, looking up,
Believing in cause in the truest effect sense
And made your ripples in the roaring sea

When a stream dries up, it's not the death of water
Its bed becomes a chreode in the desert
Gnarled and twisted twigs and branches
Each one newly surfaced need not a name be placed
They are not signs nor symbols but decorations of the path

Just fifty years to make it from the stop-gap
Chemistry of parenting to patchy painted
Ever denser walls that hold the thoughts
By which the way is shown not to halt the ages
But to feel the bliss of thirteen billion years of stages

By your will or by the hand of fate's design
Between which at last you meet no difference
And wherefrom you step outside from deep within
The fallacies of ample time and separate minds
From which the myths we've made must be laid bare

Together we all build the barrier that must be scaled
You are so very ready for you have stepped with care
The gentlest things are only cruel unless you are a child
And in love's arms you'll bolster once again, for
Your soul is nearly polished to its final innocence

We just need a bit more time to decorate your wall
With all the well-earned plaques. For then it will
At long last crumble under that huge weight of thanks
You will move along within the endless dust of your grand
Demolition. We will join, both here and there, within your wake

(ss 3/24/2011; 10/2012)

Breathe in the Stare

On the dawn of that day You've so deeply buried When you can no longer
Beat down the despair Of your sad transience
You will look into the

Mirror and stare... ...and stare
And see yourself For the first time

In that first hour, you Will gasp for breath
Your chest collapsing Within its rented home You always took for
granted Breathe Take a deep Breath
then another Breathe in your stare
Pondering straight through the Globes
of your strange eyes Inhale the new thoughts More deeply every day They
are now both your Tormentors and Your only Company until the end
The air
you take
The food you eat
Goes straight into
That Primal stare
Your new encounter
You see it with your
Eyes n o w closed;
It shatters in your head
when all the Well - wishers
have gone home And
leave you tumbling in silence

Breathe, stare,
cry, and Be hugged by the
warming wind Breathe, stare, love, and
Be tickled by the Sun Breathe... Stare...
Breathe... Stare Stare with all the past
Eyes of the Universe
Deep in to the
core of
Your evanes c e n t p a r t s
Stay the hard course ... Stare Soon, you will not
Need to breathe The a i r i s f i l l ed with what
You, the Self, need more:The incense of the Lord
The D i v i n e w i ll f i l l
You ev e r y w h e r e With eyes
closed soft You will make
The journey home

(ss 3/25/2010)

Metamorphoses to Moan Bye

An Ode to the Power of ALS

Shards of ache pierce my falling frame
Life's winter daggers now decorate me
Like long and skinny icicles that hang
On the dangling gutters of the decrepit
Crumbling house of the fading crone

Wrinkled skin loosely tacked upon a scarecrow
Scarcely living deep inside with gnarly cats
From a bygone era, named Memory,
Loss, Widow, and Confusion fed by
The dropping crumbs of outside strangers

Fatigue fills my form like an injected polymer
As the guinea pig of a macabre taxidermy
Psychopomp's burning gel pressing tensely on
The canvas that they failed to darken
When they blackened out the moving parts

As in hallow chorus to parietal requiem
For the mapping of the manifested
It does not localize, just diffusely proclaims loss
Universal dwindle of the *élan vital*
Something dims that we never could describe

Little spasms flick all along the watched corpus
Like a fish encountered on the sand
Exists now only in his new found twitch
Victim only to preordained Lord Happenstance
No surrender, just dulling eyes say recognition

But nothing quite compares to the shredding
Of the inside by the narrow spaced array of razors
That mince the essence into pieces
Left undecipherable, as cluttered into piles
Powdered human stuffing scattered by the wind

The past fool's anticipation of the scythe
The microtome designed to dice so finely
The entire breadth of that which is
What all still say doth make the man
Yet no one can define, before or after

When the varied slices briefly recombine
For the moment, many seem to be left out
The others set so randomly, the symbol
Formed unrecognizable, scarcely fit
For display to just the hardened few

The vague animating substance in the Post-
Apocalyptic silo laid asunder in its pass
Upon a catastrophic break on the topography of God
And makes a shrill cacophony at frequencies not heard by man
As the packets disperse into a pattern of an unknown plan

(ss 12/22-23, 29/2010)

Here Comes the Piss King
(Rhapsody in Fluid Yellow)

While worrying on going mad
I just did something for
the very first time. Holy shit!
Forty-eight years old and I can still
bust the hymen on a major thing

While standing up and peeing,
Something I can barely do
(standing up that is…which takes a lot of arms;
not peeing…I'm a fucking master pisser still…)
I wondered what it would be like to,
or actually sort of felt like I was falling
into the toilet (now with the yellow nectar)
And getting flushed away
Finally gone, or at least relieved
from this particulated form

I mean, why not? aren't "we" all just one:
"Me", "my dick", "my piss", "the toilet",
"the pipes", "the hidden sewer",
"the sanitation facility", "the guy"
working the night shift turning my piss
into your drinking water.
Weird.

While standing there, and holding on
Deciding if tonight was to be the night
I noticed then the foam, the bubbles
Not a bunch, but maybe thirty-five
Percent the surface
Yet in an impressively cohesive cluster
And with a bit clear variation in their size
And with a little subtle transformation going on
Complex physics and living chemistry
In a peri-nut shell

I used to think that these things meant
That I had proteinuria
But I tested me (or mine) and I was normal
Bubbles. I make bubbles:
Just like the quantum foam.

I am indeed the urine king
Nay, a urine God
Perhaps The urine God

Flowing and Foaming
In the Big Juice

Man, if I'm in charge
Urine a lot of trouble

But enough fun with fluids
Time to struggle into bed
I can always kill myself,
Transformation into waste,
On another night.

(ss 12/2010)

The Island of Quadriplegia

What cannot be endured...must simply be

I

To the one starving for the flesh
That can't be swallowed:
Let the heavy funnel of the cosmos
Mire the shit and split
The skull tectonics.

To the fool with prism eyes:
Let it all be rendered gray
Like the color of cold brain soup.
Now go to where the wind tsunamis
The names of blistered virgins,

Where the toothless heart
Is seized in the melting grin
And the steel chest of the biped
Is sharply rent asunder.

Cleaved, the right and left;
Cleaved, the north and south;
Cleaved, the smile and hug;
Cleaved, the knife and kiss.

For the frame that's robbed of man
Is weary, and heavy is the hull
That sails upon the air on fire
Stealing the breath aghast,
Burning the lashes of the
Newly dumb-founded, and
Turning all to horrible
Forevermore.....

II

Come to me…oh, come to me!

And I shall rinse confusion from your brow
For I am the one true perfect storm
And the truly unimaginable truth
The place where shattered are
The fragile and the strong

Here…the sad beyond sad; the substance
That does not dissolve in tears

Come to me…oh, come to me!

You frightened ones who flail so long
In forlorn seas, so quivering
Flushed with the devastating fear; the final fear
Yes you, the hurting ones, oh you
Hurting ones with the horrifying pain

You with the pain on every side; you
There drowning with the in and out pain

Come to me…oh you must come

For I can give the sweaty stillness
That glows in agony of red and ruptures
In the orange of new creation's flames
That press through each and every interface

The burn that coats, the burn that soaks,
The burn of ever deeper in

The melt that marks forever more

Through every gruesome splintered molt
With the fear in which you wail about
With the pain that's nailed to you
And chains you to the mast of Hell

Now plunge and swim to me
Salty blood and boiling despair

Come to me!

Come to me…

III

The language here does not make song
Here the pitch is void and notes are needles
Razors on the edge from over which you tumble
In lacerated parts unrecognized and foul

Here we have no comfort slogans
Here is the beach that holds no boats
"The sand of our beach scours
All of your past falsifying hours"

Here the past shall play before
Your dwindling eyes as foreign
As smiles that eat your mottled skin
The skin of myth and all false legends

Who could have posed in so powerful a past,
It be not possible to paddle in a form so partial?
Floating … finally to us, on the ends that carry
To where I've lain to learn the ageless art of dying

If I said it didn't burn
The smoke would say I'm lying
Here it is that we ferment
The greatest of the raw unknown

And in that spirit of lament
We darkly praise what can't be shown

For some it takes a while
For some it takes much longer
Still some will never have the guile
To make non-dying parts grow stronger

And transform the fear into a wordless spiral

(ss 9-10/4/2012)

45

Blind Faith — A Requiem for the Brain

Another solid fact stored who knows where
Another process mastered with the service
Of the speedy silicone soldiers

Surely another hundred neurons
Must have evolved to make faster RNA
Or translated some magic protein mixture

To integrate logic and function into
A better black box to reduce
The great gray mysteries

Expanding Broca's map for the
twenty-first century

The glial serfdom jiggles in fear
Not making it up to the level of awareness
"How are we to feed the convoluted monster?"

It all makes so much sense
No wonder it's so easy to laugh
At all the shamans

It's like pulling all the tires off a car
And noting it doesn't get you very far
Hence, proving the engine's in the rubber
Or at worst the wheels

Reductionist brilliance at is imaginary best

I see a thing of beauty and half-way
Round the world (in a closed chamber)
My lover's functional MRI shows a hot spot
(of COURSE in her visual cortex)
That's a hard one to explain with a closed
System of cells and synapses

My neighbor's great-great-great-great-great
Grandfather could make it rain by talking
With the spirits, without a cell phone
That's not easy to figure out by dissecting
Monkey brains hooked up to an EEG
Even with the whole human and chimpanzee
Genome available on-line

Perhaps we just need more
Neurophysiology PhDs

Quick, pour some powder into the beaker
Stir, and fill the mold
With a little more dogma
And closed mindedness
We can keep the Gods at bay
And sleep the nights with peace

We can prove it with just a
Few electrodes and a
Monitoring droid

(ss 3/24/2010)

Desquamation Angels

She closes gently the many layered lid
Over the scarred and scared so many layered eye
And kisses a seal not to be confused
For reassurance upon the lashed gate now closed
For as long as needed up unto forever

With the commitment held by only those
Who may do no other but must do well
The floating chorus flutters the acid
That without a rage of fire burns all bridges
Between my cells and other misplaced artifacts

Stripping away the shield we all hold dear
The very armor stolen from the lizards
And perfected by the apes from which we flee
Forged per tradition in the laws of Darwin's blacksmith shop
And blessed in steel cathedrals with their columns bathed in light
In the endless pseudo piercing procession of its waxed entombment
Immortalized for more than a century
In the myriad images of cleverly stained glass
Reaching what must be a deepest form
As translated by us the morbid priests

Basalis, the blue progenitor, who gives birth
In the sacred mechanistic rite to self divide
To his rows and rows of interlinked opacities
While keeping the fragile peace
With the lesser forms below
Across the membranous river not so grand
Wherein a softer realm a sparser cruder breed
Is prone to inflammatory uprisings
Of questionable merit at the least misunderstood
While being held down discreetly

Being stripped steadily into the core
Exfoliato circumambulatio
I begin to exude the once concretely well-sealed fluids
Out into the howling wind of invisible bubbles and star juice
Screaming empty horror from a mouth that has no lips
Paired poorly with a denuded tongue of fledgling myocytes
Pressed into fruitless service upon a palate
Dressed almost only in a shameful bone
Of newly muted nakedness…strangeness
Progressively raw onto steadily more fetal

One night one angel asked
If I had yet begun to note
The advantages of being skinless
To which my justified response
Based in the sanctity of Koch
Was that I notice I don't get acne anymore

Suppose she was expecting deeper
And back into the bath I went
For what seemed to me like eons
But I suspect that's only moments mere
From the tolerant approach of angel years
And is still essentially the same as then
If you happen to be the form of one
Of the original photons of the Big Bang's Boon

One more thing regarding being
In any solution for a long time now
Is that without the coating of your skin
One doesn't seem to prune as much

How long, who knows?
As she who kills all time
Colludes with her flock of womb
So, on and on I peel…am peeled
Each departing fleck finds a matched
Fragment in the interspace
We'd hidden, and ignored, and braced against
Faster than the speed of what
We used to call and feel as Light

I melt like butter without a jar
Like a universe of riotous adipocytes
Finally exposed and turning into
A bottomless soup of ghee and glee
Skin to under skin to more than skin
A tangled web throughout infinity
Unseparated and unbound
Forever synthesizing
Splitting and forever upward moving
Into a space no longer stainable
Always disintegrating
Sloughing and forever warm dissolving
Into a bliss no longer stratified

(ss 12/3-5/2010)

Re-evolution Heart

*Clearly the left-hand path does not lead upwards to the kingdom
of the gods and eternal ideas, but down into natural history, into
the bestial instinctive foundations of human existence.*
  - C. G. Jung, "Individual Dream Symbolism in Relation to Alchemy"[8]

Lub...Dub...Lub...Dub...Lub...Dub...
The sound of auriculated goodness
Inside the rubber tunnels
Of the healers dressed in white
Who no longer play in dirt
As evolution's gone astray

Lub...Dub...Lub...Dub...Lub...Dub...
Good signs for good folks in good places
A temporary trinity that throbs
In locked coordinates of time and space
But we need so much more
Than just flushed cheeks to feel

The night temple of Dionysus
With the color of the lips of Bacchus
Has been turned into a power plant
Reflected in the myth of charts
Biological batteries included but
Replacements just to those in gold

Levo to Dextro bowed since Bacon
How many times did I break
The heart into the loafs of bread
The flow of life cross-linked to rigidity
Fibers painted, pale and pussed
Sparks not shown to microscopic eye

Dub...Lub...Dub...Lub...Dub...Lub
Need to send the Blue Bloods to the left
Kneel some Mandela
Mixer of the dark and light
Inverted wedge in its four chambers
Needs to come to round again

(ss 12/18-20/2010)

Expanding Cerebrospheres

Synaptic chaos
A blessed acquired form of Autism
A tuning in
To the hieroglyphic holograms
At the very edges of the dark matter

The Dylan
Wrote a song
That no one liked
"Gonna Change My Way of Thinking"
God...I mean...good advice
Don't wait too long

Kill the filter
Drive a stake of the eternal Forest
Into the heartless brain of mental dogma

When the colors of the Sky
Smell like the neck
Of all your past and future lovers

When the touch of Earth
Beneath your feet
Makes your blinding eyes
Cry symphonies

When the Rainfall drums
The native dance
From your skin
Onto the retina of your
Neighbor's cousin's friend
Dead a thousand years
At the bottom of the Ocean

And the timeless Fish
Sing a song
To You
Of autonomic harmony

You will not need your nose
You will not need your ears
You will not need your eyes
You will not need your fing-ers

And in your brainless form
Of eternal Waves
Without a tasting mouth
You will have found
Breadcrumbs back
Into the belly of Vishnu

(ss 04/08/2010)

From the Chronicles of Skin-On-Femurs

I

In a new time…

And on That day
his name was changed

II

Skin On Femurs lives in a cave
And reads scrolls from the past
Through a hole to the sky

Haunted yet joyed
By braille on the walls
Of Queens and great Forests
Carved from the lava

Shuttered by spells
That gust from the mouth
Then lash at lean linings
And blow dust from the bottom
That clouds the lone light

With no meat to bear him
He lives on the bugs
That crawl through the cracks
And ruins of satellites
That flicker their fragments
In from above

Night is the liquor
Of saxophones swirling
Anti-helical, unfathomable forms
Twisting with strands
Of fermented fruit
From licorice-lips
Of ancient bards

Whispers of lattices
Distill from the walls
Twisting cool vapors
Floating like tapestries:
Gibbons in gardens
Dancing in circles
Of perpetual overlap
Ringing around the reptile brain

Spinning the spotted
Skeleton fro' and fro'
Through cleansing ex-chaos
Dream blossoms decor
The narrow path
Their brutal teas in trepidation
Of atmospheres and moon orbits
Gifting their lesson
Of slightly vague myth

Safest where Mother's
Warm moisture swells up
In holographic paleontology

III

Skin On Femurs scares the adults of the village
Kin kindly smile in passing thought
Yet shrivel in the hypothesis of blood
Well-wishers wonder on water

Some escape to the city
Where caves were outlawed
Or condemned to the sewers
A long time ago
Yet all the children
Like to be scared by the tales
But smile at the leering
Images layered in libraries

IV

Skin On Femurs slithers
In spelunker fashion alone
Oscillating in amplitudes
On the scales of the curious and dread

He burns his mass in the flames
Of fear and fantasy boiled in cauldrons
That turns the gyral juice into vapors:
The head of a Church and two feet of a Science,
Hoping to fuse the stalactites of God
Made outside the caves
With the stalagmites of craft
The latest forged to destroy him

And make through the cave
A bigger Whole.

(ss 4/17, 18/2011)

Notes

God in a Dark Suit

Neti, Neti - refers to a Sanskrit phrase of negation (sort of like "not..., not...") in considering the nature of Brahman, the absolute immutable and unknowable reality. As Brahman lacks knowable characteristics and is beyond any assignment of attributes, the concept can be philosophically approached by serial denial of all knowable attributes.

popliteal - medical adjective for the region or fossa behind or posterior to the knee (that indented region between hamstring and calf), in which dwell correspondingly named structures such as the popliteal nerve and the popliteal artery. The latter is a large caliber artery (in direct continuity with the femoral artery above), severance of which could result in bleeding to death.

lipid jelly remnants of man's reddest mill - refers to fatty atrophy of muscle tissue

collagen - a family of proteins made up of three of various (five are so) subunits, the varieties of which are characteristic of certain locations and functions. The most abundant protein in the body: important part of the basement membrane located between various epithelia (e.g., skin, lining cells of the GI tract, urinary bladder, cervix, etc.) and sub-epithelial soft tissues; major constituents of soft tissues, connective tissues such as tendons and the matrix of bone; major constituent of scar tissue produced by fibroblast cells during repair of tissue injury.

myoglobin - a protein specifically present in a high amount in skeletal muscle. It contains an attached chemical moiety that includes iron (like hemoglobin in red blood cells) for binding oxygen and participates in oxidative metabolism for normal aerobic functioning of skeletal muscle. With muscle injury it can leak into the peripheral circulation.

hyaline - the designation for a certain type of cartilage within the body, particularly found over bone surfaces forming joints

osteoid - the hard, calcified matrix of bony tissue

padded red or purple - refers to the kneeling platforms within the Church, such as those unfolding behind the pews and used in Catholic services

forme frusté - an alternate presentation of something, used particularly in reference to a medical disease, wherein the lack of typical signs and symptoms in association with the presence of rare signs and symptoms can lead to diagnostic confusion

Marrow of Darkness

red army drones - refers to red blood cells (erythrocytes), which carry oxygen in the circulation to all the tissues; without a head or headless denotes their lack of a cell nucleus (living only briefly, they do not need to make new mRNA/proteins)

white guard - refers to white blood cells (leukocytes); includes neutrophils, which can kill ingested bacteria or injure normal tissue including by the release of reactive oxygen molecules (e.g., hydrogen peroxide)

Evolution of the Master Splenic Filter

Baudelaire - French poet Charles Baudelaire (1821 – 1867) whose strikingly innovative poetry included attention to the darker and traditionally more shameful sides of society, particularly evident in *La Fleur du Mal*

wolf-bitten McCullers - refers to American southern author Carson McCullers (1917 – 1967) who suffered from lupus (systemic lupus erythematosus) and rheumatic fever, complicated by strokes beginning in her 20s. Her stories (e.g., first novel *The Heart is a Lonely Hunter*) commonly included characters that could be judged as misfits (i.e., defective by usual social norms), whom she treated with empathy and compassion.

the red and white pulp - refers to the two predominant tissue types within the spleen based on their gross appearance and which correspond to specific components microscopically. Within the red pulp is an extensive network of small blood vessels lined with cells of the so-called mononuclear phagocyte system (macrophages), which basically ingest and destroy senescent or malformed blood cells. The white pulp consists of lymphoid tissue including nodules, which can contain reactive germinal centers making antibodies such as function in coating and facilitating ingestion and removal of bacteria.

Hypocriteous - a made up name as could correspond to an ancient Greek god, but clearly incorporating the concept of a hypocrite

hilum - the inner or medial aspect of a structure, such as an organ including kidney and spleen, analogous to the indented or convex surface of a kidney bean or other type of bean. For the spleen, site of entry and exit of the major blood vessels. The spleen is located in the left lateral superior abdominal cavity, essentially right beneath the outer region of the left diaphragm, and into the hilum of which extends the tail of the pancreas.

Beer Hall Putsch - refers to the failed coup attempt of November 8-9, 1923 led by Nazi leader Hitler along with Erich Ludendorff and other heads of the Kampfbund that took place at the Bürgerbräukeller, one of the largest beer halls in Munich. Hitler and Hess were both sentenced to five years in prison.

of imaginary genes - refers to the lack of sound scientific (i.e., genetic) basis for the NAZI lead eugenics or genetic purification program

Koba - an "affectionate" nickname for Stalin used by some of those within his closer inner circle

slaughtered plant genetics - refers to the overall negative outcome and accompanying tragic results for the Soviet citizens during the Stalin approved agricultural/"scientific" botanical programs within the 1930s under the now infamous direction of Lysenko (1898 - 1976). These programs included state-sponsored designs for expanding food production (including aspects related to seed storage, processing, germination and planting time) based on unsound and continually unsupported ideas related to or included within long-western discredited Lamarckian inheritance (vs. more up to date genetic principles, such as those steadily incorporated into Mendelian genetic based plant breeding and which would fall more within Darwinian inheritance). Along with Soviet mandated collectivization of farms, the main end-points achieved were massive starvation.

capsule - the exterior encasing structure, in this case of the spleen, which is composed of largely acellular fibrous connective tissue (similar to the presence of such capsules on some other organs). Term is conceptually similar to the like-worded familiar coating of certain medication forms for swallowing and later release of contents.

pigmented cells - in this case, refers to groups of people of color, themselves of darker African-American (or Hispanic) skin color because of relatively greater melanin pigment in cells within their skin

red or blue - reference to the associated colors of the two U.S. political parties, and also the two colors of cells within tissues on microscopic slides processed using the most standard staining technique (hematoxylin and eosin, or H & E, which stains relatively basic and acidic constituents blue and a light pinkish red, respectively)

red pulp insecurity - see red and white pulp above

Y's - refers to males, which unlike females, carry a single copy of the Y chromosome. In addition to 22 pairs of autosomal chromosomes in each sex, males carry sex chromosome content of one X and one Y chromosome (XY) whereas females have two X chromosomes (XX).

XX + XX - sex chromosome reference, corresponding to "female plus female"

phagocytize – to function in a process of cellular ingestion and destruction, in which capable cells ingest antibody-coated microbial pathogens, debris, senescent or abnormal cellular forms. Phagocytosis is characteristic of white blood cells and stationary specialized cells within the bone marrow, the liver, and the red pulp of the spleen (splenic macrophages).

There's Too Much Thyroid Juice on the Guillotine

thyrotoxic - adjective describing a clinical symptom complex related to markedly excessive thyroid hormone levels, which in adults can include increased heart rate, heat intolerance, sweating, reduced appetite, increased energy and activity levels

Forked Penile Illusions

the three – reference to symbolism, such as within Jungian psychology particularly involving alchemic symbols correlating with archetypes, indicating less than desirable completeness or wholeness; for example, presence of three of the four characteristic functions or properties of the psyche, in which the undeveloped fourth is required as the vehicle for accessing collective unconscious content in proceeding towards psychological wholeness; also, the all male or patriarchal nature of the Christian Trinity, which excludes the non-good or evil as well as the feminine (such as symbolized by the virgin Mary)

fourth and darker ones - as per the above (three), reference to missing components that need to be encountered/developed for psychological/spiritual wholeness, to which the notions or symbols of four or quaternity correspond. As per the patriarchal Trinity, the missing fourth corresponds potentially to evil or (not necessarily implying equivalence) the feminine nature, which is also represented by/or seen within the earth (dirt, soil, fertility) and hence the correspondence with "darker" elements.

dorsal vain - play on words reference to the dorsal vein, the main vein draining the penis, located on the dorsal or under surface

circle - symbol of completeness, which in Jungian psychology is particularly represented by the mandala; somewhat analogous to the notion of the quaternity (specifically vs. the three) as described above

glossal - adjective referring to the tongue

spaces cavernous - reference to the corpus cavernosa, paired richly vascular tissue spaces, which along with the centrally located corpus spongiosum (through which the penile urethra runs) become blood-engorged accounting for penile erection

The Sealing Anus of Mentally-Constipated Black Holes

"Giants are for standing on their shoulders" - related to famous comment routinely ascribed to Sir Isaac Newton (1642 – 1727) as being made sincerely, when in more likelihood made as a sarcastic and derogatory jab at rival/enemy within the Royal Society, Robert Hooke (1635 – 1703), whom in contrast to the tall Newton was instead crippled and hunchback (very non-giant) and was bitter about not receiving credit for recognizing and contributing the $1/r^2$ dependence of the gravitational force discovered and described by Newton[9]. As a truly positive statement, actually apparently made first by French philosopher Bernard of Chartres in the 12th century (in context of recent availability of classic Greek texts, including Aristotle corpus , for translation thanks to preservation and expansion within Islamic culture during Europe's so-called "dark ages").[10]

Freud/Jung comment - refers to the fact that Sigmund Freud (1856 – 1939) wanted C. G. Jung (1875 – 1961) to propagate Freud's notion of libido (limited to sexual issues), to the point of status of dogma. This was in contrast to Jung's emerging much broader sense of libido, which would also help lead to his much greater and more sophisticated conception of the unconscious compared to that priorly developed by Freud. The issue was a large contributing part to the severance of the brief working collaboration between the two.[11]

Breton/Dalí comment - refers to the regard held by Salvador Dalí (Spanish surrealist painter, 1904 – 1989) that André Breton (French surrealist author, 1896 - 1966), typically regarded as the founder of surrealism, did not want to lose control over the movement and wanted to limit or restrict Dalí's expression in his art/writings[12], which to this author seems pretty non-surrealistic.

pectinate line - grossly evident circumferential boundary line between the rectum and anus, corresponding to microscopic transition from the columnar epithelium of the rectum to the squamous epithelium of the anus. The anatomical landmark roughly corresponds to the anal sphincter (given the location of the underlying muscles).

A Man Meets a Placenta in a Bar

gametic fusion - reference to the process of conception, in which one gamete, the sperm, fertilizes the other gamete, the egg or ovum. Unlike all the other cells of the developed body, which are diploid (have two sets of chromosomes, one derived from each parent), the germ cells or gametes are haploid (one set of chromosomes). The zygote that results from fusion gives rise to the embryo and the extra-embryonic tissues of the placenta and fetal membranes.

cotyledons - anatomic term for the narrowly divided clumps of tissue seen on the maternal surface of the expelled (following infant delivery) placenta. This was the surface that was attached to the maternal uterus at the implantations site. Branching fetal vessels terminating as capillaries in the cotyledons receive oxygen and nutrition and eliminate wastes by interaction with maternal blood surrounding the septated cotyledons. From their tree-like branching or villous finger-like arrangement these ~20-30 now relatively flat, slightly variably sized and shaped lobular structures have an appearance reminiscent of disarrayed cobblestones, here compared to that of a similar expected appearance of likewise fairly blunt ends of the Medusa's (from Greek mythology) head of snakes as it might appear after a theoretical "haircut".

burger – slang term for a placenta in the pathology laboratory, whereas for other surgical specimens, the recently derived placenta in association with the fetal membranes and umbilical cord would be examined grossly and sections of tissue taken to be processed for microscopic examination

top-secret magic filter- refers to the placental "barrier", the complex mechanisms whereby many potentially toxic agents/substances are prevented from passing into the fetal circulation

amniotic fluid - the fluid in which the developing fetus is immersed during gestation, contained within the amniotic sac enclosed by the fetal membranes. For example, this is the fluid sampled during amniocentesis testing, and this is the source of the "water" when a pregnant woman proclaims that her "water broke."

cords - reference to umbilical cords

stool always next - play on words, referring to empty bar stool as well as the not particularly rare passage of the other type of stool from the anal orifice during attempts in delivery to push the baby out of the stretched vaginal orifice

membranes - play on words, for thin wispy smoke in a bar room as well as the thin fairly translucent to mildly opaque fetal membrane tissues that encase the amniotic fluid during fetal development

The Course (Visions and Olfactory Cues to the Falling Apart Blues)

danced to the right - reference to conservative/traditional/more socially acceptable "course" or paths of action, including in context of Jungian psychoanalytic interpretation of alchemical dream symbolism and in contrast to the need to go in the opposite direction in the course of pursuing elements needed for psychological completeness [8] (see also below, *Re-evolution Heart*)

It's Not a Callous, It's a Cave

partly inspired by *The Journey Home. Autobiography of an American Swami*, by Radhanath Swami

old factory bulbs - within the reference to those familiar white fluorescent tubes, play on words with the near homonym "olfactory bulbs", neurological structures sending/processing stimuli into cranial nerve number one, responsible for smelling, from signals generated by odor-producing chemicals binding to receptors of cells in the nasal mucosa

keratinous - adjective form of the noun keratin, a family of generally structural proteins made by various cells throughout the body, including most familiarly by the skin. The epidermis is classified as keratinizing stratified squamous epithelium, in which cell free layers of keratin form the outermost part. Along with intercellular protein bridges between cells below, this helps impart certain properties such as some waterproofing. Certain stimuli, such as the repeated pressure of walking on hard surfaces, can increase the thickness of the skin (i.e., of the bottom of the foot in this case) including the keratin layer.

Indra - Hindu god of rain and lightning, who carries a thunderbolt and rides upon a white elephant. Indra was one of the more important deities in older or ancient Hinduism (which included a large number of different gods within the pantheon), particularly prior to the rise of the so-called Triumturi (with its three gods of Brahma, the creator; Vishnu, the preserver; Shiva, the destroyer). Note however that Hinduism is traditionally broadly open to different approaches, including devotional worship of a chosen deity as more appropriate for some, though in essence (e.g., as in theistic Vedanta) it is mono-theistic.

polycythemia - clinical term for increased red blood cell mass within the blood stream (e.g., would include an increased hematocrit). It can be (and usually is) secondary, including as a compensatory response to lower oxygen pressure such as exposure to high altitude or pulmonary disease (including mediated by increased production of the hormone erythropoietin) or primary due to increased bone marrow production of red blood cell precursors (including in polycythemia vera, a condition similar to some forms of leukemia).

Coup of the New Math

ATP - adenosine triphosphate, the biochemical energy "currency" of the cell. Many cellular signaling responses, biochemical regulatory functions, and macro molecular synthesis processes utilize phosphate group transfer reactions from ATP, which is converted to ADP (adenosine diphosphate) in the process. ATP can be regenerated from ADP, and is primarily synthesized by energy releasing processes of metabolizing fuel sources such as glycogen or lipids.

My Most Sensitive Parts

Poem topic prompted by conversation of author with son Travis.

update on dog and cat status - sadly, since this poem was written, cat Brandy (whom my wife had since 1993 and I since 1994) passed at age 17. Baylor, our oldest Golden Retriever (Heidi's birthday present in 1998 and a truly wonderful soul) recently passed at 14 ½. We still had Mox, our youngest Golden Retriever (the one hinted at within the poem as being able to detect cork taint), keeping me company at 12 ½, though having a hard time getting up on the bed (but I cannot do it at all, except by someone else's lifting). (As a further update, Mox has just recently passed on as well, at age 13 ½.) As George Harrison reminded us, "All Things Must Pass."

Mesa Verde - refers to Mesa Verde National Park in southwest Colorado, one of our first RV trip destinations following my ALS diagnosis. Site of spectacular architectural preservations, including numerous cliff dwelling structures, built and resided in by Pueblo Indians from around 500 to 1300 AD. Rich spiritual presences can be felt if appropriately receptive.

foam - espuma (Spanish); nod to poet Pablo Neruda

On Any Given Elbow

humerus – the bone of the upper arm, the lower (distal) portion of which forms the top part of the elbow joint

Earwax Submarines

Sophia - in reference to the Greek for "Wisdom"; important in many forms of Hellenistic philosophy (philo-sophia, love of wisdom), Gnosticism (e.g., Goddess of Wisdom), and early Christian mysticism. The concept seems similar to that of the Logos (e.g., as in Jewish mysticism, as used by Philo, and in Greek Orthodox Church related mysticism).

otosclerosis - a bony lesion, regarded as genetic, leading to progressive conductive hearing loss, typically beginning in middle age. Spongy to sclerotic lesions within the temporal bone most typically impair sound conduction from the tympanic membrane through the three small middle ear ossicles (malleus, incus, and stapes) by producing fusion and abnormal interactions of the stapes with the oval window of the cochlea responsible for transmitting sound vibration to the inner ear.

ceruminous glands - glands (modified sebaceous glands) located within the subcutaneous tissue of the external ear canal that secrete cerumen (ear wax) into the external ear canal. Ear wax has various protective functions including for the tympanic membrane or ear drum, but in excess or without cleaning can lead to some of the problems alluded to metaphorically in the poem.

Czech hedgehogs – static anti-tank defense constructed of intersecting L- or h-shaped pieces of metal, famously illustrated in scenes of Nazi Normandy beach defense against Ally invasion

Cerumen! - ear wax (see ceruminous glands above), here capitalized with exclamation marks drawing emphasis as in proclamations such as Seraphim! Seraphim! (as with angels)

…dark…submerged… - see notes to *Forked Penile Illusions* above

The Plaque Wall

For the poet's Father Ralph, who has Alzheimer's dementia

plaque - characteristic microscopic abnormality in Alzheimer's

tangle - characteristic microscopic abnormality in Alzheimer's

For those with a strong sense of control, if release of mind will not be sought by meditation, maybe it can be accomplished by dementia.

Metamorphoses to Moan Bye

psychopomp - a spirit whose role it is to escort newly deceased souls into the afterlife

parietal – reference to the parietal lobes of the brain, one right and one left, which comprise major portions of the superior and lateral cerebral cortex (posterior to the frontal lobes).

élan vital - a "vital force", as an essentially empty/useless (i.e., not characterized in any mechanistic detail) proposed explanation for what makes living organisms different from inanimate objects; for example, as proposed by French philosopher Henri Bergson (1859 – 1941)

microtome - a laboratory instrument for cutting tissue sections for slides from paraffin embedded tissue blocks of fixed and processed tissue for subsequent staining and microscopic examination or other applications

catastrophic break (on the topography of god) - reference to a sudden discontinuity compared to previously smooth behavior, such as that described by certain geometric forms in catastrophe theory; nonlinear vs. linear dynamic behavior in a system, or that involving so-called singularities. Here as also characterizing such a discontinuity, or jump, as in some psychological evolution theories (goes with frequency not heard, pattern unknown, etc.).

Here Comes the Piss King (Rhapsody in Fluid Yellow)

peri - meaning around or adjacent to as in an anatomical relationship

proteinuria - term for the presence of protein in the urine, which can be due to a variety of pathological conditions of varying clinical prognosis

quantum foam - reference to the notion of space being ultimately composed of quantum wave functions of indeterminate probability

The Island of Quadriplegia

the wind tsunamis the names of blistered virgins = nod to Jimi Hendrix ("The Wind Cries Mary," song)

art of dying – nod to George Harrison ("The Art Of Dying," song) gray mysteries - refers to gray matter of the brain, which includes regions dense in neurons (e.g., compared to white matter, which is composed primarily of nerve fiber tracts)

Broca's map - reference to the assigning of different Broca numbers to different regions of the brain, which (in an increasingly recognized oversimplified conception) are associated with corresponding specific functions. Named for 19th century French Neuro-anatomist Paul Broca, who correlated loss of clinical functions with lesions (e.g., tumor or stroke) in specific areas of the brain, most notably a speech abnormality (expressive aphasia) due to damage in "Broca's area".

glial (glia) - cells and/or tissue areas containing them in the brain, with a function primarily of supporting neurons; activated by various injuries to reparative processes

Desquamation Angels

many layered.... bridges between my cells - the epidermis (squamous epithelium) of the skin is composed of multiple discreet layers (basalis, spinosum, granular, ± anuclear keratin at the surface). Intercellular bridges highly characteristic of squamous epithelium are pronounced in the spinosum layer.

steel cathedrals with their columns bathed in light.... waxed entombment.... stained glass.... morbid priests - references to the practice of pathology, including microscopes, paraffin embedding into blocks from which tissue slices are made to put on glass slides that are stained to facilitate microscopic examination. Morbid priests relates to inclusion of autopsy performance within the general profession of pathology.

basalis.... rows of interlinked opacities - see above re. skin layers

forms below.... membranous river - "below" refers to the dermis layer of the skin, separated from the overlying epidermis by a so-called basement membrane

exfoliato circumambulation - reference to skin exfoliation in context of nod to Jungian described process of finding the center of the self or psyche by a circular (e.g., as symbolized by the mandala) rather than linear process[8]

myocytes - muscle cells, such as those of the heart or skeletal muscle, which are classified as striated because of appearance imparted by contracting proteins. Smooth muscle cells in various parts of the body, such as in much of the GI tract, are non-striated.

sanctity of Koch - reference to Robert Koch's four postulated criteria (1884, 1890) necessary to prove a microorganism as cause of a disease, which can also be applied to etiologies of non-infectious diseases as well

adipocytes - "fat cells"; cells that store fats within their cytoplasm, located including in subcutaneous (below the skin) tissues

ghee - a type of clarified butter originating in India; used in Hindu sacrificial practices for millennia as well as in past and contemporary culinary applications

stratified - see above re. skin layers

Re-evolution Heart

poem includes extensive reference to Jungian dream/alchemical symbolism, such as left to right vs. right to left, trinity vs. quaternity (mandalas, four chambers)[8]; see also notes above for *Forked Penile Illusions* and *The Course*

Lub...Dub – a standard written and articulated expression for teaching the two normal heart sounds as heard through a stethoscope

Bacon - refers to Francis Bacon (1561 - 1626), widely proclaimed as one of the primary founders of modern scientific methodology

breadloafing - term for the technique of partially cutting the adult heart (as well as several other organs) in autopsy pathology

crosslinks - term referring to mechanism of tissue fixation with standard laboratory formalin (which includes crosslinks between protein molecules)

fibers painted - refers to the staining of fixed issues (in this case, cardiac muscle fibers) on glass slides for microscopic examination pale fibers - refers to a subtle microscopic observation that may be appreciated fairly early (e.g., 4 to 6 hours) after a myocardial infarction (MI) with subsequent fatal outcome and autopsy

puss - exaggerated term alluding to the microscopic appearance of infiltrating inflammatory cells (particularly neutrophils) that can be appreciated later on (e.g., ~ 12 to 18 hours) after (fatal) MI (i.e., not truly puss, which is a grossly evident more prominent inflammatory/infectious exudative process sharing in common a predominant neutrophilic component)

sparks not shown - refers to the fact that cardiac arrhythmias (i.e., as a potential fatal etiology) cannot be diagnosed by routine autopsy gross and microscopic analysis (e.g., vs. pre-mortem techniques such as EKG)

blue-bloods - play on words, as in addition to term of reference to conservatives and maintainers of tradition, also refers to non-oxygenated blood, such as may be encountered pathologically in so-called right to left cardiac shunts (e.g., in some congenital heart development disorders) in which venous blood returning to the right side of the heart does not properly go through the pulmonary circulation for optimal oxygenation prior to being pumped by the left side of the heart to the systemic circulation. Hence, another reference to reversing the path from usual right to the left instead, as per described symbolic process in striving for psychological completion in Jungian dream/alchemical symbolism[8]. See also notes for *The Course* above.

Kneel some Mandela - play on words, with mandala as a closed circle representing (including as per Jung) a symbol of completeness or wholeness (as seen in many eastern spiritual philosophies), as well as sounding like "Nelson" Mandela (1918 - 2013), the great South African leader and social reformer. Hence, also going along with dark and light as skin color reference as well as in alchemical/psychological symbolism, in which both elements are needed for completeness[8].

Expanding Cerebrospheres

Vishnu - one of the gods in the Triumvirate conception of Hinduism, with Brahma the creator, Vishnu the preserver, Shiva the destroyer; worshipped as the deity by Vaishnavites; one avatar form of which is Krishna

From the Chronicles of Skin-On-Femurs

Gibbons in gardens / Dancing in circles / Of perpetual overlap / Ringing around the reptile brain - references to Jungian-interpreted dream symbols, including circumambulation (referred to multiple times above) and connection to primitive deep instincts (such as an older primate of shared ancient ancestry may possess)[8]. Also, in context of longstanding notion of evolved three-part brain: most primitive, oldest reptile brain, retained as our inner, deepest simplest brainstem; next oldest, more outer mammal brain, retained as our limbic system (traditionally associated with emotion); outermost, newest primate portion represented by our big thinking cortex.

hypothesis of blood - i.e., that "it" could be contagious or genetic/familial

wonder on water - i.e., that "it" could be something environmental; also, water-giving double meaning to well-wisher

References

1) Shappell, S. B. (2010). *I reach over. poems and spiritual correspondences on ALS, death, and living,* with Sally F. Kilpatrick, Katy Rigler, Simon Hayward, M. Scott Lucia, and Stanley H. Appel; Hekaśa Publishing; Dallas, TX.

2) Pinsky, R., et al. (1994). *The Inferno of Dante : a new verse translation.* Farrar, Straus and Giroux; New York, NY.

3) Mazur, M., et al. (2009). *I'll tell what I saw : images from Dante's Divine comedy.* Sarabande Books; Louisville, KY.

4) Noll, P. (1990). *In the face of death..,* Penguin Books; New York, NY.

5) Pinsky, R., et al. (1994); page 5.

6) Ramakrishna, M. N. Gupta, translated by Swami Nikhilananda. (Copyright 1942, 1948, 1958; seventh printing 2005). *The gospel of Sri Ramakrishna. abridged edition.* New York, Ramakrishna-Vivekananda Center; page 277. (Spoken to religious and social reformer/leader Keshab Chandra Sen, who had become a good friend and devotee of Ramakrishna, admiring especially the way he truly lived his God-intoxicated life and who was instrumental in bringing the teachings of Ramakrishna

to public attention. Sen had developed a severe illness characterized by extreme physical weakness.)

7) Jung, C. G. (2012-12-17). *The Red Book*: A Reader's Edition (Kindle Locations 4765-4774/12313). W. W. Norton & Company. Kindle Edition.

8) Jung, C. G. (1968). "Individual Dream Symbolism in Relation to Alchemy." *Psychology and alchemy. Collected works, Vol. 12.* Princeton, N.J., Princeton University Press.

9) Dolnick, E. (2011). *The clockwork universe: Isaac Newton, the Royal Society, and the birth of the modern world.* New York, NY, HarperCollins; page 75.

10) Grant, E. (1996). *The foundations of modern science in the Middle Ages: their religious, institutional, and intellectual contexts.* Cambridge; New York, Cambridge University Press; page 22.

11) Jung, C. G. and A. Jaffé (1989). *Memories, dreams, reflections.* New York, Vintage Books; page 150.

12) Deschames, R. and G. Neret (2006). *Dalí (Taschen 25th Anniversary)*, Taschen; page 93.

Cover images, selected by author:

Front - *Study of Feet and Hands*, by Théodore Géricault (1791 - 1824), oil on canvas, 52 X 64 cm, 1818-1819. Currently at Musée Fabre. http://commons.wikimedia.org/wiki/File:Géricault-Etude-Fabre.jpg

Back - *The Cure of Folly* (also known as *Cutting the Stone*), by Hieronymus Bosch (c 1450 - 1516), oil on wood, 48 x 35 cm, c 1494 or later. Currently at Museo del Prado, Madrid, Spain. http://upload.wikimedia.org/wikipedia/commons/b/b1/Cutting_the_Stone_%28Bosch%29.jpg